DISNEY

FROZEN

THE ESSENTIAL GUIDE

Disney

FROZEN

THE ESSENTIAL GUIDE

Written by Barbara Bazaldua

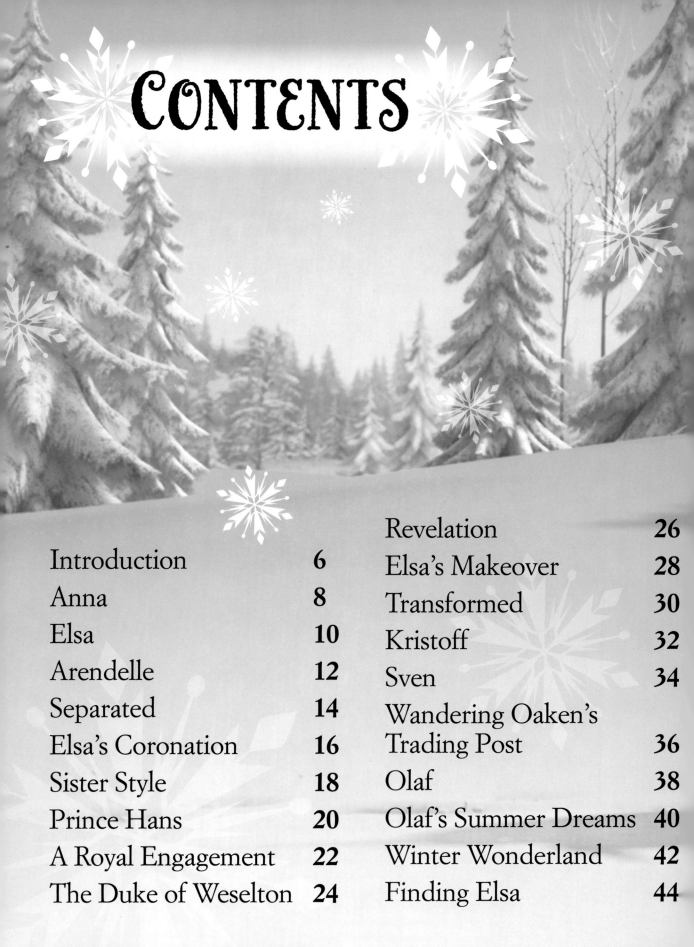

CONTENTS

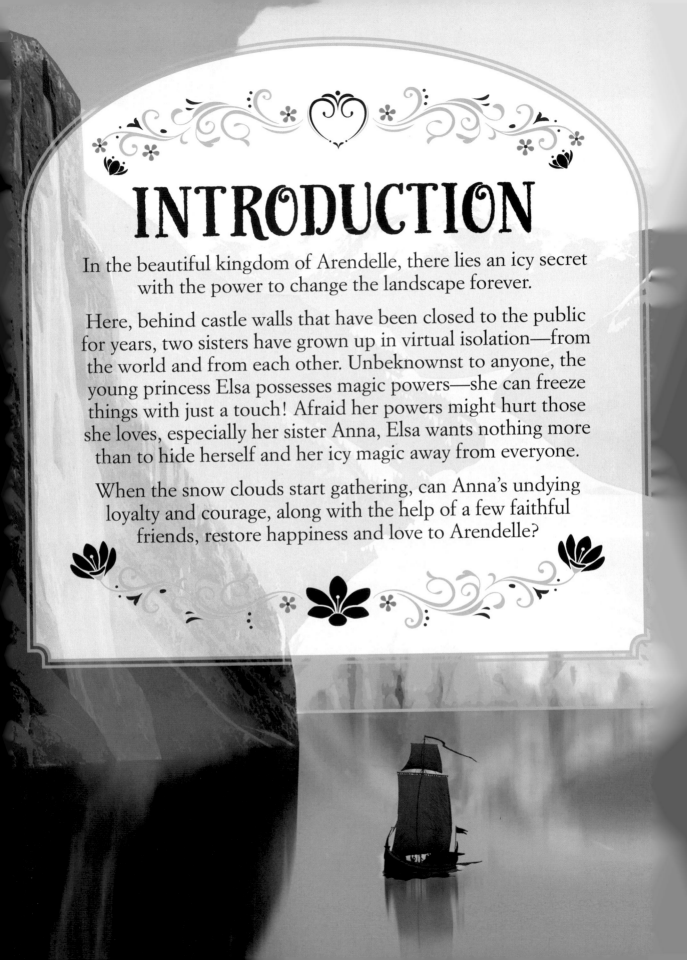

INTRODUCTION

In the beautiful kingdom of Arendelle, there lies an icy secret with the power to change the landscape forever.

Here, behind castle walls that have been closed to the public for years, two sisters have grown up in virtual isolation—from the world and from each other. Unbeknownst to anyone, the young princess Elsa possesses magic powers—she can freeze things with just a touch! Afraid her powers might hurt those she loves, especially her sister Anna, Elsa wants nothing more than to hide herself and her icy magic away from everyone.

When the snow clouds start gathering, can Anna's undying loyalty and courage, along with the help of a few faithful friends, restore happiness and love to Arendelle?

ANNA

Princess Anna of Arendelle is more daring than graceful, more playful than poised, and more caring than careful. She is hurt when her older sister Elsa starts ignoring her, and doesn't understand the reasons for Elsa's new, strange, behavior. More than anything, Anna wishes they could be close again.

Uh… hello?

When Anna first meets a charming prince at the docks, she is awkward and unsure what to say. She is not used to talking to strangers— especially dashing, handsome ones.

Forgotten childhood

Anna has no idea that Elsa, now the new Queen of Arendelle, is shutting her out in order to protect her, or even that Elsa has any secrets to hide. Will this new change in their lives help them to reconnect?

"I am so ready for a change!"

Strand of white hair caused by Elsa's secret icy powers

Brave and bold

When things go wrong, loyal Anna is willing to bravely face darkness and cold to save her sister and make things right. She is determined to never give up.

Act first, think later

This cheerful princess is bubbling with energy and zest and longs to experience life. A bit impetuous, she rushes headfirst into things—often without considering the consequences ahead of time.

DID YOU KNOW?

One of Anna's favorite desserts is krumkake—a thin waffle-like cookie shaped like an ice-cream cone and stuffed with sweet fillings. Yum!

Sturdy boots for daring adventures

ELSA

The beautiful, elegant princess Elsa was born with icy magic. When she accidentally injures her sister Anna, she must learn to control her powers. To do this, she believes she must hide her emotions—including her love for Anna. Elsa's chilly poise hides the fact that she is frightened—of herself and what she can do.

Father's daughter

After her parents' sudden and tragic deaths at sea, Elsa knows she must take to the throne when she is 21. On her coronation day, she gazes at her father's kingly portrait, hoping she can be as wise and generous a ruler as he was.

Secret keeper

Strong emotions, such as those triggered by a row with her sister, can cause icy outbursts. When Elsa accidentally freezes the village fountain, her secret is out and the villagers are confused. Is their beloved new queen a wicked sorceress?

True or False?

Elsa likes keeping the secret of her powers from Anna.

False—she feels like she has no other choice.

"Control it. Don't feel. Don't let it show."

Regal posture

Stormy outlook

Shutting herself away from other people soon turns out to be not such a good idea. Elsa had hoped to protect people, but she ends up sending a snow storm over Arendelle that she has no idea how to stop.

Who needs warmth with clothes this cool?

Snow queen

After her coronation, Elsa flees to the mountains, where she feels free to be herself and unleash her powers at last. She says she doesn't care what others think, even when she is called a monster. Can this new feeling of freedom last?

Gown woven of ice and snow

ARENDELLE

The kingdom of Arendelle is a prosperous place, gleaming like a jewel between a sparkling fjord and shining, snow-capped mountains. For Elsa's coronation, and for the first time in years, the doors of the castle have been opened to guests and the public. Welcome!

Down at the docks

People arriving to trade with or visit Arendelle often come by boat from across the fjord. On the morning of the coronation, guests arrive from kingdoms far and wide. Anna is excited to meet new people, and rushes down to see the crowds.

From the castle balcony, Elsa can look down on the kingdom that is now hers.

No laughter has echoed in the castle for years. That all changes when the rooms are opened for the arriving guests, and a grand ball is held in the lavishly decorated ballroom!

Arendelle's happy inhabitants love the royal family. They gather in the marketplace to greet their new queen.

Magical land

Arendelle is surrounded by majestic mountain peaks, vast forests full of woodland creatures and mythical beings such as trolls, and deep fjords that bring ships from afar. Anna wishes she could explore all of it, if only she had more time!

Arendelle's beautiful fjords shine silver in the moonlight. The water can be crossed via a wide arching bridge. It makes for a romantic setting.

SEPARATED

As little girls, Elsa and Anna aren't just sisters, they are playmates and best friends. Anna loves playing with Elsa—especially when Elsa uses her magic to make exciting things happen!

"Do the magic!"—Anna

Elsa, busy creating a blizzard in the ballroom

Magical playground

If you could create snow like Elsa, what would you do? Build snowmen anytime you want? Slide down slippery slopes in your own living room? It sounds like cool fun, doesn't it? For Elsa and Anna it is a daily reality!

An icy accident

Elsa's magic is fun, but also dangerous. One night, Elsa's powers hit Anna in the head. The king and queen rush Anna to the trolls, who have healing powers. In order to save her, they remove her memories—Anna no longer remembers Elsa's magic, just the fun they once shared.

Anna, ready for action!

Knock, knock

Anna doesn't understand that Elsa has shut herself away because she is scared she may hurt Anna again. Anna knocks and knocks, but Elsa's door stays closed. Without her sister, Anna is lonely and bored. Losing her best friend hurts.

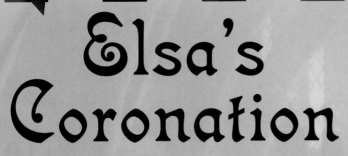

Elsa's Coronation

On Elsa's coronation day, the castle gates are opened for the first time in years and people fill the marketplace, singing, dancing, and cheering for their beautiful new queen.

Crowning moment

As the coronation ceremony begins, Elsa seems calm and poised. But inside she is afraid. Can she control her powers? Today of all days she needs to remember her parents' lessons to conceal and not feel.

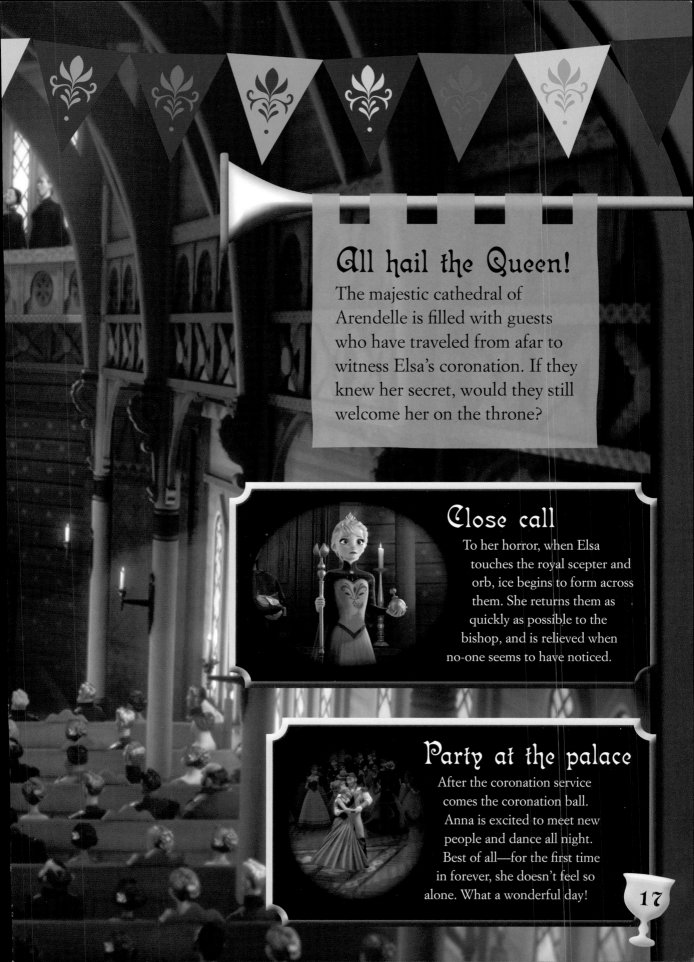

All hail the Queen!

The majestic cathedral of Arendelle is filled with guests who have traveled from afar to witness Elsa's coronation. If they knew her secret, would they still welcome her on the throne?

Close call

To her horror, when Elsa touches the royal scepter and orb, ice begins to form across them. She returns them as quickly as possible to the bishop, and is relieved when no-one seems to have noticed.

Party at the palace

After the coronation service comes the coronation ball. Anna is excited to meet new people and dance all night. Best of all—for the first time in forever, she doesn't feel so alone. What a wonderful day!

SISTER STYLE

The two young princesses have very different personalities. While Elsa seems perfectly poised, Anna is desperate for adventure. Can the two ever learn to get along? Inside, these girls are both caring, compassionate, and generous— and love each other deeply.

Elsa would prefer to stay locked away in the castle forever. But this is only because she loves her sister and doesn't want to hurt her.

Other people may complain about cold weather—but not Elsa! She loves snowy winter days—bring on the snowmen!

The new queen has a great sense of fashion and style. Elegance is always Elsa's first choice. And sparkles don't hurt either.

Elsa is a natural leader, but worries about the responsibilities that come with being ruler. If she could learn to relax, she would be ok!

ELSA

Cheeky Anna loves to play around and act silly. Others enjoy her sense of humor. She can always make them smile.

Anna is naturally adventurous, and longs to know what lies beyond the castle walls. She's ready to seize any opportunity she's given to meet new people!

Despite being the youngest, Anna is very brave and will do anything to help friends and family. But sometimes she leaps before she looks.

Although she likes dressing up in fancy clothes, Anna's favorite outfits are casual and comfy so she can move freely around the castle!

ANNA

PRINCE HANS

The perfect picture of a prince, Hans is strong, smart, and ever so handsome. Perfectly groomed from his boots to his shirt buttons, fun-loving Hans looks like he stepped out of a book on how to behave royally. No wonder Anna falls for him. He is just so charming!

Sharp uniform for wowing princesses

First impressions

At first, Hans thinks Anna is just a simple, but cute, villager girl. When he learns that she is Princess Anna, he bows gallantly. That's how to impress a princess.

In search of a kingdom

Hans has a grand total of 12 older princely brothers. At least a few of them ignored his existence for years at a time. No wonder Hans wants to find someplace where he feels like he really belongs. He comes to Arendelle with hopes of finding the key to his future.

Perfectly polished for seeing own reflection

"I've been searching my whole life to find my own place."

DID YOU KNOW?

Anna thinks Hans' last name is "of the Southern Isles." But of course, that is just where his home kingdom is.

Stargazers

After growing up feeling rejected by their families, Hans and Anna feel like they have a lot in common. Hans promises Anna he will never shut her out. But is that how he really feels?

Rescue party

When Anna goes after Elsa and does not return, Hans bravely volunteers to ride to her rescue. He is even prepared to face Elsa and her terrifying icy powers.

A ROYAL ENGAGEMENT

As Anna and Hans talk, laugh and skip through the kingdom, she soon discovers tha they have so much in common, they could even finish each other's... sandwiches.

Fun and games

As they slide down the polished castle halls, Hans tells Anna he loves acting crazy. After years of loneliness, Anna loves finding someone to laugh and act silly with.

Starry eyed

Gazing into each other's eyes, Anna and Hans feel as if they've discovered something they've never felt before. They agree—it must be true love!

Happy time

Standing on the ledge of the town clock, Anna and Hans laugh as they mimic the clockwork figures' mechanical movements. Time flies when you're having fun!

Magic in the air

Gazing at the moon and stars, Anna and Hans make a promise to get married. They both believe that they have discovered their place in the world—with each other. But will everyone else be as happy about it as they are? What will Elsa think about their hasty engagement?

THE DUKE OF WESELTON

The arrogant Duke of Weselton may be small, but he packs a lot of scheming into his scrawny body. All he wants is to get his gloved hands on Arendelle's riches. At first he appears charming and overly friendly, but no one should trust him further than they could throw him.

Gruesome twosome

The Duke has two thugs who do whatever he asks of them. After Elsa flees, he sends them after her and instructs them to put an end to the winter—whatever it takes. The duo are foolish enough to think it will be easy.

Honored guest

The Duke of Weselton looks like he is one of the most attentive guests at Queen Elsa's coronation ceremony. However, he is actually happily thinking of the riches he will have when they become closer trading partners.

Mustache
for hiding
scheming
smile

"Open those gates so I may unlock your secrets and exploit your riches."

Fancy clothes for
looking important

Weasel of Weselton

From the nearby kingdom of Weselton—not to be pronounced "weasel town"—the pompous and vain Duke thinks he can out-dance, out-charm, and out-wit anyone. He may try to ooze charm and grace, but all he really oozes is slyness and greed.

Sorcery!

When Elsa turns the village fountain to ice, the Duke accuses her of cursing Arendelle. Does he believe what he is saying, or is he just grabbing his chance to get the upper hand?

True or False?

The Duke loves to show off his dancing skills.

True—too bad he doesn't have any.

Skinny legs
for weird
dance moves

REVELATION

When Elsa hears about Anna and Hans' engagement, she is frustrated, but she tries to keep calm and not argue with her sister. However, Anna gets upset and pulls off one of Elsa's gloves, revealing Elsa's powers. Elsa runs from the castle, but as she touches the village fountain, it turns to ice. Her secret is now well and truly out.

Good news?

Anna assumed Elsa would be overjoyed to hear about her engagement to Prince Hans. But cautious Elsa cannot believe anyone could fall in love so fast, and forbids their marriage.

Shocked faces of Arendelle villagers

Without her gloves, Elsa finds it much more difficult to control her powers.

A cold trail

Anna didn't mean to upset Elsa with news of her engagement, or for Elsa to freeze summer. In fact, she didn't even know about Elsa's powers. She goes to find her, hoping to make everything right.

Marketplace fountain, frozen mid-flow

Monster or misunderstood?

With the crowd closing in, Elsa believes she has no one who will help her. She is wrong. She has Anna. If only Elsa would listen to her sister. Accused of sorcery by the Duke of Weselton, Elsa is afraid she will not be able to control her powers and flees.

ELSA'S MAKEOVER

Once Elsa flees up into the mountains, she is free at last to be herself and reveal her powers. What better time to have a makeover? She was always elegant, but now her true self is reflected in her new look and her icy surroundings. The Elsa that was crowned Queen of Arendelle has been left far behind...

Up on the North Mountain, Elsa enjoys designing unique and playful patterns in the snow and ice, and discovering how powerful her magic can be.

Elsa's tightly coiled hair is now a loose, flowing braid, and her sparkling new gown shimmers and floats like snowflakes on the wind.

Using her powers, Elsa builds a magnificent ice palace that shines brightly against the snow-capped mountain top.

As Elsa climbs up the mountain, she creates a staircase of ice beneath her feet, rising higher with each step she takes.

29

TRANSFORMED

High in the mountains, Elsa has called forth a winter storm and, without the fear of hurting others, is enjoying the freedom to let loose her full powers. Leaving Arendelle far behind her, she is unaware that she has left her kingdom locked in an eternal winter. Anna believes Elsa will unlock the spell—but can she? Does she even know how?

Silently and swiftly, thick sheets of ice sweep across the fjord, imprisoning ships in an iron-cold grip. The coronation guests fear they will be stuck in Arendelle forever!

The North Mountain, where Elsa creates her ice palace.

Snow continues to fall as Elsa's magic appears unstoppable.

Snow blankets the mountains and turns the forests into wonderlands of glittering icicles. Traveling will be tricky for Anna as she sets out to find her sister.

In Arendelle, the villagers panic. They are used to cold and snow—but not in summer!

Frozen Arendelle

From the height of summer, Arendelle has been rapidly transformed. The residents and coronation guests are trapped as the fjord freezes over, and in their hour of crisis, they turn to Prince Hans to help them.

KRISTOFF

A strong outdoorsman, Kristoff Bjorgman is also a hard-working ice cutter who knows how to survive. No-nonsense Kristoff follows his own rules and doesn't care what others think. But underneath that rough 'n' tough exterior beats the heart of a romantic softie.

Reindeer serenade

At the end of a long, cold day, Kristoff relaxes by serenading his best reindeer friend Sven with his lute and a song. Sven appreciates Kristoff's talent— but he might be the only one!

True or False?

Kristoff loves the winter Elsa has created.

False—he sells ice and no one wants to sip cold drinks now!

thick animal hide jerkin— comfortable, but not stylish.

"I don't take people places!"

Mountain man

Kristoff has spent most of his life up in the mountains, with Sven and the wise old trolls for company. From them he has learnt lots about love, but never experienced it himself. Anna's courageous optimism might be just what he needs to brighten up his life.

Tall, strong, and frosty

The sudden change in weather is not good for Kristoff's ice business. Perhaps that's why he is so grumpy when he first meets Anna. Her request for a lift on his sled to find Elsa does not go down well—he just wants to be left alone!

Gloves protect fingers from freezing

Hero's ride

When Kristoff lets his feelings for Anna take the reins, he bravely rides to her rescue, breaking records for downhill reindeer racing on his way.

No slipping and sliding in these shoes!

SVEN

As loyal and playful as a very big puppy, Sven is Kristoff's best friend and faithful companion. Big, fast, and strong, Sven can pull Kristoff's sleigh over vast distances. The romping reindeer is always up for a game of fetch—especially if it involves carrots.

Antlers for poking Kristoff

Says who?

Sven is a very rare breed of reindeer—he can talk! Well, actually, Kristoff pretends to speak for him. Sven thinks it is silly. Surely he wouldn't sound that goofy?

Nuts about noses

Sven thinks Olaf the snowman is very likeable—especially his nose. Although the two become pals, Sven can't help wanting to get his chompers on it. Crunch!

DID YOU KNOW?

Olaf mistakenly thinks both Sven and Kristoff are called "Sven." This doesn't bother Sven, but Kristoff dislikes being likened to a "donkey."

Dinner time

Stuck in Oaken's barn for the night with nothing to eat, Kristoff finds that the carrots Anna brings make a pretty good dinner. Sven could have told him that.

Wags tail like a dog when happy

A man's best friend

Kristoff rescued Sven when he was a young fawn and they have been as close as two peas in a pod ever since. Sven acts as Kristoff's conscience, using snorts and antler pokes to make him do the right thing—including rushing to Anna's rescue when she needs a friend.

Wide hooves for trampling in snow

WANDERING OAKEN'S TRADING POST

Set deep in the forest, Wandering Oaken's Trading Post offers weary woodsmen and other travelers a place to get what they need. It also serves as home for proprietor Oaken, who lives there with his family. Oaken never worries about competition from other stores— because there aren't any others for miles around.

It may be cold outside, but inside it is warm and toasty, especially with the roaring fire and sauna out back.

Summer sale

Jolly shopkeeper Oaken prides himself on knowing what his shoppers want. So he was ready for summer with swimsuits and suntan lotion made from his own recipe. But he never expected the weather to change so suddenly. Anyone for sunbathing in the snow?

Snowy shoppers

As Anna looks for warm clothes
so she can continue her quest to find
Elsa, Kristoff stomps into the store.
The snow-coated ice seller needs
carrots and other stuff. But he
is short on money and long on
attitude—and that's not going to
buy him any special deals from Oaken.

Wooden troll
carvings guard
the door to
Oaken's store.

Oaken sells
many curiosities,
for all weathers
and occasions.

A humble haven

Searching for her sister, Anna trudges
through the snowy forest, feeling more and
more like an icicle with each step. Then she
sees lights glowing from Oaken's Trading
Post. It is a simple log cabin with a barn
and sauna, but Anna is so cold, it looks as
welcoming and grand as a castle to her.

OLAF

If you could have a snowman for a friend, Olaf is the one you'd want! A warm-hearted little snowball of fun, he loves life and is ready to try anything. Eager, curious, and trusting, Olaf sees the best in everyone and in every situation, and he is always willing to lend a stick hand to help others.

Excited to meet you!

Olaf is so excited about making new friends that he loses his head. Luckily, he can plop it right back on. And his smile is just as bright upside down.

Bringing back summer

Olaf is desperate to experience summer. So when Anna explains that finding Elsa will end the big freeze, Olaf happily offers to take them to her. Warm days coming up!

DID YOU KNOW?

Elsa used her special icy powers to make Olaf. Anna remembers playing with him back in happier times, when Elsa used to create wintery wonderlands for fun.

"I'm Olaf, and I like warm hugs!"

Olaf's head comes off—a lot!

Stick arms for hugging.

Carrot nose, provided by Anna and Kristoff.

Wise friend

Olaf is smarter than he looks. When he tells Anna that true love is putting someone else's needs before your own, it's enough to melt anyone's heart!

Fresh face

Helping is one of Olaf's favorite things. Sadly, most people are alarmed at the sight of a walking, talking, dancing snowman! Olaf is thrilled when he meets Anna and Kristoff, especially when they provide him with a new nose. But he'll have to keep Sven from munching it!

In hot water

Olaf thinks soaking in a hot tub would melt his cares away. He doesn't know what happens to frozen water when it gets warm! (It's s'no fun!)

Beach buddy

Getting gorgeously tanned at the beach sounds great to Olaf. Just once, he'd like to be a sandman instead of a snowman!

Olaf's Summer Dreams

Olaf dreams of fun in the summer sun. How cool would it be to feel warm? There is just one problem: he has no idea what happens when snow meets heat. In his vision of summer, he would be free to dance and sunbathe all day long...

"I've always loved the idea of summer and all things hot!"

Happy tappin'

Just thinking about summertime makes Olaf feel like dancing. In his imaginings, the seagulls also catch his rhythm. Watch those feet fly!

Cold reality

Even a snowman has dreams. No one wants to ruin Olaf's hopes that someday he'll have a chance to experience summer—with the harsh truth that he would turn to slush!

Who turned off the water?

Where's the sound of rushing water? It seems Elsa's freezing powers can even stop a thundering waterfall in mid-plunge. Now, it's one big sheet of ice.

Tricky terrain

The sudden change in season is trickier for some than others. But for a snowman, it's perfect—as Olaf proves by cheerfully belly surfing down the slippery slopes!

Dreamland

Journeying to the North Mountain to find her sister, Anna and her new traveling companions see another side of Elsa's powers—the new wintery landscape shines more brightly than any winter they have ever seen before.

Ice rink

Sven's hooves are made for walking in snow, not sliding on ice. He wants to stand up, but his legs have other ideas. Too bad reindeer don't wear ice skates.

WINTER WONDERLAND

Who knew winter could be so beautiful? Elsa's winter might have the villagers shivering and shaking in their boots, and may have ruined Kristoff's ice business, but here the woods gleam with icy magic.

43

FINDING ELSA

Anna has battled wolves and climbed icy cliffs to find Elsa, but now she faces her toughest challenge—breaking through the walls in her sister's heart. Anna pleads with Elsa, reminding her that they were once close and could be again. But Elsa believes that Anna, and everyone she cares about, will be safer if she stays away.

When Anna begs Elsa to return and break the spell that holds Arendelle in endless winter, Elsa is disturbed. Causing the snow storm was easy, but she doesn't know how to make it stop!

Elsa battles to control her emotions—and fails. Icy power bursts from her body. Watch out, Anna!

The inside of Elsa's ice palace reveals an intricate ice staircase and stunningly beautiful towering walls.

Chilly confrontation

Now that Anna knows Elsa's secret, so much about their childhood makes sense! Ever-hopeful Anna sees no reason why Elsa cannot return to Arendelle, but Elsa does not agree. Their argument leads to Elsa accidentally blasting Anna with her powers, and then banishing her from her ice palace.

MARSHMALLOW

Formed by Elsa's powers, Marshmallow is her loyal snow-guard and always does her bidding. Agile, fast, and strong, Marshmallow is nice enough at first—until he becomes angry. That's when his spikes pop out and he turns extra fiesty! Marshmallow is dedicated to protecting Elsa and her ice palace. He loves his job!

Spikes pop out when angry

"Go home! Don't come back!"

Icicle fangs

Powerful stompin trompin' f

True or False?

Marshmallow is afraid of fire.

True—just like Olaf, Marshmallow risks melting if he steps too close to anything hot.

Silent type

Marshmallow is very different from Elsa's other living snow creation—Olaf. The massive Marshmallow doesn't talk much, but he doesn't have to. One look at his spiky fists and cavernous mouth and no one hangs around for a friendly chat.

Monster menace

Marshmallow is first summoned to escort Anna and Kristoff from Elsa's ice palace. But Anna throws a snowball at the big guy, which makes him *really* mad. The friends race away, but Marshmallow is as unstoppable as an avalanche. Run!

Snow on snow

When Olaf bravely tries to stop Marshmallow so his friends can escape, the big bouncer puts the squeeze on him. Is Olaf about to be turned into snowballs?

FEAR VS. LOVE

Before Anna arrived, Elsa's ice palace was a place of refuge, where she could be herself and enjoy her powers. She thought that she could flee from her responsibilities in Arendelle without there being any consequences. But Anna made her think twice about her choices. And in the meantime, Elsa has done the one thing she feared the most—hurt the sister she loves.

A long drop

When Anna refuses to leave Elsa's ice palace without her, Elsa orders her bulky bodyguard, Marshmallow, to escort Anna and her friends out. Talk about getting the cold shoulder.

Secret orders

Leading his men against Elsa in her ice palace, Hans is determined to rescue Anna, not knowing she has already left. But the Duke of Weselton's two thugs have different orders from their boss: destroy Elsa.

All alone

She may have
seemed cold and
uncaring when she told
Anna to leave, but grief and
pain batter Elsa's heart. She is
sure sending Anna away was
right. It was also one of the
hardest things she has
ever done.

49

THE TROLLS

Have a problem with uncontrollable powers or the state of your heart? Ask a troll for help. When Elsa's powers accidentally hurt Anna for a second time, the trolls know what to do. The droll creatures are happy to give advice, and their ancient wisdom is worth listening to. Some of them are older than the boulders themselves.

Anyone searching for advice needs to act fast—the trolls turn to stone when the sun comes up.

"Only an act of true love can thaw a frozen heart."

The youngest trolls are particularly excited to see their old friend Kristoff.

50

"The **heart** is not so easily changed, but the **head** can be persuaded."

Matchmakers

When Kristoff tells Anna he has friends who are experts in love, he means the trolls, who befriended him when he was a child. The trolls love making matches and have been trying to find the perfect partner for Kristoff for years. They think Anna is just the girl!

True or False?
Trolls don't live for very long.

False—Hulda is 700 years young, and Pabbie is not telling anyone his age!

EPIC JOURNEY

Some journeys change you forever. Although they are far from friends at first, as Anna and Kristoff travel to rescue Elsa, they experience danger, beauty, and fun—and discover something neither of them expected.

Frosty beginnings

When they first meet, Kristoff thinks Anna is bossy and stubborn. Anna thinks Kristoff is rude and *more* stubborn. Gradually they learn to stop arguing and work like a team.

Left hanging

The intrepid explorers are soon forced to trust each other. After reaching Elsa's ice palace, they are chased off a cliff by Marshmallow, where they are soon out of rope. Will the snow cushion their fall? Only one way to find out—let go!

Friend's farewell

Thinking Anna will be safe with Hans, Kristoff bids farewell. He is not sad. He believes this is best for Anna, and he is fine being alone—right? Or has the journey ended with him loving Anna?

Race against time

Following the trolls' advice, Kristoff carries Anna in his arms and races toward Arendelle so Hans' kiss of true love can keep her from freezing forever. But she grows colder every moment—faster, Sven... faster!

ce breaker

...ver underestimate
...power of white hot
...mixed with ice cold
...nation. Furious and
...ful, Elsa's powers are
...ut to break down
...ery walls of her
...cell, allowing
...r to escape.

IMPRISONED

Despite Elsa's powers, Hans manages to capture her and bring her back to Arendelle. Now she is a prisoner in her own castle. With no idea where Anna is, or that her magic fatally struck Anna in the heart, Elsa's fear makes the snow storm worse. Hans says he'll try to help her and plead her case to the dignitaries who want to get rid of her. But can she trust him?

Not even a prison can contain Elsa's magic. Elsa is alone and upset, and pretty soon frost begins to creep up the walls.

Final warning

Hans asks Elsa to bring back summer, but Elsa tells him she doesn't know how! Hans thinks he holds all the power, but he is forgetting what Elsa can do with her bare hands.

Even though her wrists are trapped inside iron shackles, Elsa's emotions cause her powers to burst out and free her.

True Love

When Anna first set out on her journey to rescue Elsa, she thought she knew what true love looked like. But she soon realizes it's not all moonlight and romance. When the trolls tell her she must experience an act of true love to recover from Elsa's spell, can she work out what that means before it's too late?

Prince charming

Hans sweeps Anna off her feet the moment they meet. He is handsome, fun, and sophisticated. But does she really know him? Is he really her one true love?

Pucker up!

When Anna and Kristoff hear the trolls' advice, they both assume that Anna's act of true love must be a kiss from her fiancé Hans. But what if they were wrong? What else could an act of true love look like?

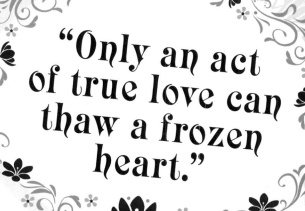

"Only an act of true love can thaw a frozen heart."

Brave heart

He may have doubted Anna's judgment to begin with, but Kristoff soon comes to admire her courage, optimism, and good humor. Above all, he bravely puts her happiness before his own.

A sister's love

True love comes in many forms. Elsa's decision to shut herself away from everyone—including Anna—may have seemed hurtful, but was motivated by simple fear. Meanwhile, Anna has always deeply loved Elsa. Will Anna have the opportunity to show her sister that love is stronger than fear?

MELTING A FROZEN HEART

Slowly becoming colder and weaker from Elsa's magic, time is running out for Anna. Unless she can decipher the trolls' advice and find her act of true love, then she will become entirely frozen and remain that way forever...

The awful truth

Back at the castle, Anna begs Hans to give her a kiss of true love to save her life. Then Hans reveals his true colors—he never really loved her. Is all hope lost for Anna? And what has Hans done with Elsa?

Race against time

As Elsa's storm grows worse, Kristoff ignores the danger and races back to save Anna. It doesn't matter whether she loves him—he loves her. He may be gruff and rough, but his heart is pure gold.

Sister act

Determined to kill Elsa and take over the kingdom, Hans chases Elsa as she flees across the frozen fjord. Meanwhile, Anna believes Kristoff may be the only one who can save her. As Anna struggles to reach him, she sees Hans raise his sword against Elsa. Anna has a choice to make: save herself or save her sister. Anna lunges in front of Hans' sword, could this act of love for her sister be the act that mends her heart?

A Tale Of Two Sisters

Once upon a time, in the kingdom of Arendelle, there lived two princesses named Elsa and Anna. They were sisters, and they loved each other dearly. But Elsa had a magical ability to create ice and snow, and she became fearful that she might accidentally hurt Anna. To protect Anna, Elsa shut herself away.

Princess Anna

Carefree young Anna didn't know about Elsa's powers. All she remembered were the happy times they had once shared. And she yearned to have them once again.

Queen Elsa

Elegant Elsa lived in fear of her own magic. The years went by, until it was time for Elsa to be crowned Queen. Anna was thrilled. In her heart, Anna hoped she and Elsa could be together again, but her head told her that Elsa wanted nothing to do with her.

Prince Hans

Hans is the handsome prince who met Anna at Elsa's coronation and told her that he wanted to marry her. But secretly he planned to take over the kingdom.

Snow storm

When Elsa's icy powers were revealed, she fled from Arendelle and built herself a palace of ice, accidentally creating eternal winter in the kingdom at the same time. Hans traveled into the mountains and brought Elsa back to Arendelle as a prisoner.

Reunited

With bravery and love Anna saved Elsa from Hans and taught her not to fear her powers, but to use them to create beauty and happiness. At last, they were together and happy again. Anna's love saved her own life and also helped Elsa see that love is stronger than fear.

GREAT THAW

Sadness turns to joy, the snow and ice fade away, and so does Elsa's fear—all thanks to Anna's bravery, loyalty and love. Whatever happens to the two sisters from now on, they will never be shut off from each other again. For them, that's enough to make the sun shine brightly ever after.

Happy days

Uh-oh! With the weather warming up, Olaf feels a little drippy. It's a good job Elsa is on hand. She uses her powers to create a mini snow cloud to hover over him and keep him cool.

A new adventure

With Anna safe, Kristoff could go back to his solitary mountain life. But he finds he doesn't want to. His adventures with Anna have led to a new adventure of the heart—and the possibility of love. Maybe reindeer aren't better than people after all.

ACKNOWLEDGMENTS

LONDON, NEW YORK,
MELBOURNE, MUNICH, AND DELHI

Editor Emma Grange
Designers Lisa Robb, Sam Bartlett
Senior Designer Lynne Moulding
Pre-Production Producer Siu Chan
Senior Producer Danielle Smith
Managing Editor Laura Gilbert
Design Manager Maxine Pedliham
Art Director Ron Stobbart
Publishing Manager Julie Ferris
Publishing Director Simon Beecroft

This paperback edition published in 2014
Dorling Kindersley is represented in Canada by
Tourmaline Editions Inc.,
662 King Street West, Suite 304,
Toronto, Ontario M5V IM7

First published in the United States in 2013
013–192407–Dec/13

ISBN: 978-1-55363-250-4

Color reproduction by Altaimage in the UK.
Printed and bound in China by Hung Hing

DK would like to thank Barbara Bazaldua for her writing, Pamela Afram and
Lauren Nesworthy for their editorial assistance, and Chelsea Alon,
Rima Simonian, Winnie Ho, Laura Hitchcock, Jeff Clark and Maria Elena
Naggi, Ryan Ferguson, and Roxanna Ashton at Disney Publishing.

Discover more at
www.dk.com
www.disney.com